First Fabulous Facts

Amazing Inventions

Written by Clive Gifford
Illustrated by Patrizia Donaera
Cartoon illustrations by Jane Porter

Consultant: Adam Hart-Davis

A catalogue record for this book is available from the British Library

Published by Ladybird Books Ltd
80 Strand, London, WC2R 0RL
A Penguin Company

001
© LADYBIRD BOOKS LTD MMXV
LADYBIRD and the device of a Ladybird are trademarks of Ladybird Books Ltd

ISBN: 978-0-72329-460-3

Printed in China

Contents

What is an invention?

An invention is a new gadget or new way of doing something. An invention might be a new kind of food or medicine, a new material or a new type of machine.

chemicals

food

toys

hot-air balloon

electronics

paper clip

helicopter

Fabulous Facts

Tough job

Some inventors spend years inventing. James Dyson made over 5,000 models of his vacuum cleaner before it was ready.

No, not quite it...

A sticky idea

Velcro™ fastener

George de Mestral saw seeds sticking to fabric and discovered they had tiny hooks. It inspired his invention Velcro™, which fastens clothes.

Burst of light

American inventor Thomas Edison made over 1,000 inventions. They included microphones, light bulbs and sound recording devices.

light bulb   phonograph   microphone

Wow!

Not all inventions are successful. One of Thomas Edison's ideas was a sofa made from solid concrete!

I need a cushion!

5

Ancient inventions

People have been inventing things throughout history. Before the wheel was invented over 5,500 years ago, objects had to be dragged along the ground, or logs were sometimes used as rollers.

log rollers

wheel

Wheely good

Without the wheel, we would not have any of these things:

bicycle

trolley

pushchair

car

6

Fabulous Facts

Central heating

Wealthy ancient Romans had the first central heating! Heat was made by a furnace in the basement. The hot air flowed underneath the floor and then up through spaces between the walls.

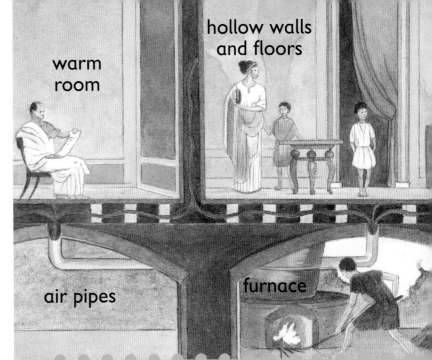

warm room

hollow walls and floors

air pipes

furnace

Whizz bang!

The first fireworks were made in ancient China, using bamboo tubes filled with gunpowder.

Ooo! Wow!

Yuck!

The ancient Egyptians made one of the first toothpastes. It was made from mashed up salt, mint leaves, flowers and pepper.

salt

mint

flowers

pepper

I'm brushing my teeth, Mummy!

On the road

Motor vehicles have engines that turn wheels round. Before they were invented people walked, rode on bicycles or horses, or used animals to pull carts and carriages along tracks and roads.

horse-drawn cart

early motor car

Fabulous Facts

Full steam ahead

The first motor vehicle was a large steam engine invented by Nicolas Cugnot in 1769. It had a top speed of just 4 kilometres (2.5 miles) an hour.

That's really slow!

On two wheels

In 1885, Gottlieb Daimler and Wilhelm Maybach built the first motorcycle out of wood. It even had wooden wheels that were covered in iron!

Seeing clearly

Early car drivers struggled to see through the rain and snow until Mary Anderson invented the first windscreen wipers in 1903.

Thanks, Mary!

Wow!

In 2013, British plumber Colin Furze invented a toilet fitted with an engine that could race at speeds up to 88 kilometres (55 miles) an hour.

Wheeee!

In the air

It took some very smart inventors to get humans into the air. The first successful powered aircraft was the Wright Flyer I, built by brothers Orville and Wilbur Wright. It flew in North Carolina, USA, in 1903.

Wright Flyer I

Wow!

In 1783, the Montgolfier brothers built the first hot-air balloon. The first passengers were a sheep, a duck and a cockerel!

I can see our farm from here!

On and under water

The first boats were large logs that were hollowed out into simple canoes, or tied together to form rafts. Since then, lots of new inventions have allowed people to travel on or under the water.

canoe

raft

Air underwater

Jacques Cousteau invented the aqualung in 1943. A tank on the diver's back feeds air to their mouth so they can breathe while underwater.

Wow!

Ralph Samuelson was just eighteen years old when he invented the first water skis in 1922.

Hi, Mum!

Communications

People communicate in lots of ways. The first writing, called cuneiform, was created over 5,000 years ago by the Sumerians. The first printing press to print books was invented in 1440 by Johannes Gutenberg.

cuneiform

printing press

Fabulous Facts

World of web

In 1991, computer scientist Tim Berners-Lee created the World Wide Web for people to share information. In 1992, there were just fifty websites. Twenty years later, there were over 630 million!

W-w-w wow!

Phone call

"Mr Watson, come here. I want to see you," were the words of the first successful telephone call. These words were spoken by the inventor, Alexander Graham Bell in 1876.

Wow!

The first mobile phone was made by Motorola™ in 1973. It weighed as much as a bag of sugar!

My arm aches!

Walk and talk

Walkie-talkies were invented for soldiers to use during the Second World War.

Computers

Computers are now common and can be taken anywhere. But only sixty years ago, they were rare and very large. One of the first computers, the ENIAC, made in 1947, filled a room bigger than a tennis court.

Fabulous Facts

Victorian computer

Mathematician Charles Babbage had an idea for a computer in 1822. He could not build his 'difference engine', but one was completed in 1991.

Computers will be...

Tail tale

The first computer mouse was invented in the 1960s by Douglas Engelbart. He called it a mouse because its cable looked like a tail.

Hey, that's me!

Wow!

The first computer bugs were actual insects that crawled inside early computers and caused them to stop working!

15

In the home

Lots of inventions have made a big difference to life at home. Appliances like washing machines and vacuum cleaners make housework easier, while food can be frozen or microwaved in an instant.

microwave,
1945

vacuum cleaner,
1905

automatic washing machine,
1937

dishwasher,
1886

What would we do without these?

Fabulous Facts

Go mow!

In 1963, Karl Dahlman built the first hover lawnmower, the Flymo™. It rode on a cushion of air like a hovercraft as its blades cut the grass.

Wheee!

Can do

Tin cans for food were invented in 1810 by Peter Durand. The can opener was not invented until 1855, so early cans had to be opened with a hammer!

I'm hungry!

Freezer food

Clarence Birdseye invented a way of freezing food quickly in 1923. Foods could now be stored and eaten all year round.

Mmmm!

Wow!

Over 6 million Roomba™ robot vacuum cleaners have been sold since their invention in 2002. This makes it the most common robot in the world!

Okay, that's enough!

Home entertainment

Lots of inventions have brought sound, images and fun into the home. One of the most popular is the television. The first TV sets went on sale in 1928, but there were almost no programmes to watch!

tiny screen

Fabulous Facts

Switching channels

The first wireless remote control for a TV was invented in 1955 by Eugene Polley. People had to press buttons on the TV to change channels before.

Spaced out

Spacewar! was the first computer action game, invented by American student, Steve Russell in 1962.

I win!

First MP3

The first MP3 player was the MPMan™ F10 invented in South Korea in 1997. It could hold around twenty songs.

MPMan F10

Wow!

An estimated 500 million people watched the first television pictures from the Moon when they were broadcast in 1969.

19

Health and hygiene

Many inventions have helped people to live more healthy lives. Some have helped us stay clean and free of disease. Others have allowed doctors to treat people's health problems.

sticking plaster, 1920

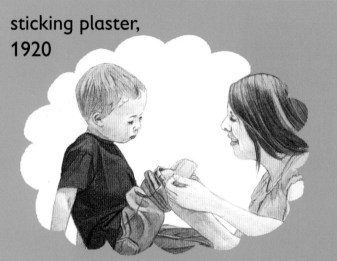

toilet paper, 1880

soap, 5,000 years ago

X-ray, 1895

What would we do without these?

Fabulous Facts

Seeing small

The microscope, which scientists use to study and cure diseases, was invented in the 1590s by Hans and Zacharias Janssen.

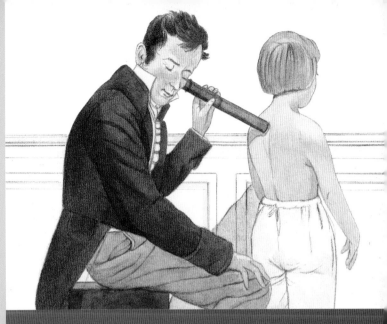

Listening in

Stethoscopes allow doctors to listen to a person's breathing and heartbeat. French doctor, Réne Laënnec invented the first stethoscope in 1816.

Wow!

At least 6.3 million kilograms of poo travels down toilets and sewer pipes in the United Kingdom every day! That's equal to around 1,000 elephants in weight. Yuck!

Poo!

21

Everyday items

Many ordinary things you take for granted and use every day without thinking are the result of inventors and their bright ideas.

paper clip

rubber band

battery

photograph

Fabulous Facts

Pen pal

In 1938, Laszlo Biro invented the first ballpoint pen. Over 100 billion of one type of biro pen, the Bic™ Cristal™, have been sold since 1950.

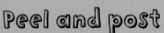

Peel and post

An attempt to make super-strong glue in 1968 created weak glue! This was put on pieces of paper that could then be stuck on and peeled off, creating the Post-it™ note.

Zip it up

It took eighty years and three different inventors before the zip became common on clothes.

Zip it!

Wow!

Famous artist and scientist Leonardo da Vinci designed an alarm clock that tickled a sleeping person's feet to wake them up.

Zzzz!

23

High-tech inventions

Electronic items, such as smartphones and tablet computers are quickly replaced by newer, better versions. Specialist technologies like robotics and 3D printing are becoming available for people to buy.

football-playing
ASIMO™ robots

Fabulous Facts

Brainy phone

The first smartphone, called 'Simon', was invented by IBM™ in 1993.

Can I speak to Simon?

Tablet tapping

The first tablet computer with a touchscreen keyboard was the GRiDPad™, invented in 1989.

Why has it got a pen?

Printing objects

A 3D printer makes objects by printing layers of material on top of each other. The first successful one was invented by Charles Hull in 1984.

Wow!

MakerBot™ 3D printer

Wow!

The world's smallest pair of glasses was made by German engineers in 2010. At only 2 millimetres wide, they would fit on a housefly's head!

I can see!

25

Inventions for fun

Not all inventions are made to solve problems or change the way things work. Some things are made to be played with, or just to make us laugh.

Flying fun

The Frisbee™ flying disc toy was invented by Fred Morrison in the USA in 1938, after he had fun throwing a pie tin.

Balloon boss

British scientist, Michael Faraday invented the rubber balloon while making equipment for serious science experiments using hydrogen gas.

Fabulous Facts

Splash happy
The first Super Soaker™ water pistol, invented by space scientist Lonnie Johnson, went on sale in 1990.

Super-soaked!

Brick by brick
Lego™ was invented in 1947 by Danish carpenter Ole Kirk Christiansen. For every person on Earth, there are eighty-six Lego bricks.

How high can I make it?

Hairy help
Harvey Adams invented the moustache cup in the 1860s. It stopped a man's moustache from drooping into his food when eating!

How splendid!

Wow!
The Barbie™ doll was invented by Ruth Handler in 1959 and named after her daughter. Over 1,000 million Barbie dolls have been sold since then.

Record breakers

Most powerful computer

The Tianhe-2 super computer was built in China and first switched on in 2013. It can do the same amount of work as over 300 million home computers!

Biggest rocket

The Saturn V was 111 metres tall and weighed more than 400 adult elephants! It launched the Apollo spacecraft, which carried the first people to the Moon in 1969.

Most common shopping invention

The bar code was invented in 1974. It is a series of black lines found on the packaging of most goods. It gives the name of the item and its price when scanned at a shop checkout.

Swimming robot

In 2012, The Wave Glider™ robot swam 14,700 kilometres across the Pacific Ocean, from the United States of America to Australia.

Row, row, row your boat

Micro micro

The Michigan Micro Mote is a complete computer on a tiny chip. Made in 2012, it measures just 1 millimetre by 1 millimetre!

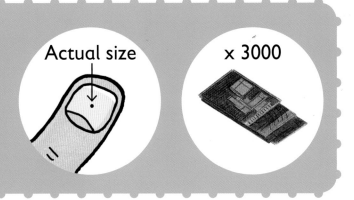

Actual size

x 3000

Invented funnies

Why did the computer squeak?

Somebody stepped on the mouse!

What do you get if you cross a dog with an aeroplane?

A jet setter!

How did the teddies keep cool?

Bear conditioning!

Why do witches fly on brooms?

Because vacuum cleaners are too heavy!

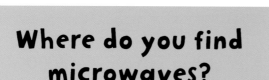

Where do you find microwaves?

On micro-beaches!

What happened to the inventor of the cannonball?

He got fired!

Glossary

applicance　　　A piece of equipment or a machine that does a special job.

communicate　　To share or pass on information, news or ideas.

computer　　　An electronic device that uses information to create a result or a solution to a problem.

electronic　　　A type of device that has microchips and other parts that control electrical currents.

engine　　　　A machine with moving parts used to make vehicles move.

gadget　　　　A small device that is especially useful or inventive.

gunpowder　　A type of explosive that is used in fireworks.

mathematician　An expert in mathematics.

MP3　　　　　A way of storing sound as a very small file that can be shared on the Internet.

smartphone　　A mobile phone that can access the Internet, take photographs and perform other tasks.

website　　　　A location connected to the Internet that contains web pages.

Index